Musical Settings
for
Noonday
and
Compline

 CHURCH

CHURCH PUBLISHING, NEW YORK

Church Publishing Incorporated
445 Fifth Avenue
New York, NY 10016

10 9 8 7 6 5 4 3 2

Contents

Acknowledgements

The settings contained in this booklet are from *The Hymnal 1982*, and are found at S 296–S 304 (Noonday), and S 321–S 337 (Compline). The hymns are reprinted from the Singers Edition of the Hymnal. Hymn numbers in parentheses refer to the proper number in the Singers Edition.

Individual copyright notices follow:

Introduction: Copyright © 1988, David Hurd.
Noonday: Setting Copyright © 1985, The Church Pension Fund.
Compline: Setting Copyright © 1985, David Hurd. Used by permission.
Hymns:
  1 (13) Words: Copyright © 1982, Charles P. Price.
  2 (15) Words: St. 3 © 1982, James Waring McCrady.
  3 (16) Words: St. 4 © 1982, Anne K. LeCroy.
  4 (18) Words: Copyright © The Church Pension Fund.
  5 (19) Words: St. 3 © 1982, James Waring McCrady.
  6 (22) Words: St. 3 © 1982, James Waring McCrady.
  7 (38) Words: St. 5 © 1982, Anne K. LeCroy.
  8 (40) Words: St. 5 © 1982, Charles P. Price.
 10 (44) Words: St. 4 © 1982, James Waring McCrady.
 11 (45) Words: St. 4 © 1982, James Waring McCrady.

Introduction

While Anglicans have long cherished the practice of reciting Morning Prayer and Evening Prayer—often with singing, the Episcopal Church increasingly has also discovered the richness of the brief noonday and late evening Offices only since forms for these services appeared in the *Book of Common Prayer,* 1979. These so called 'little offices', historically owned exclusively by set-apart religious communities, now have been claimed by the church at large. Accordingly, *The Hymnal 1982* has provided hymns and other traditional musical forms in its Appendix for the singing of these services. There are not many congregations apart from monasteries and convents where it is practical to sing the noonday and late evening Offices on a daily basis. Nonetheless, with repetition and in time, the music of these services and the practice of singing may add considerable beauty and depth of expression to the words prayed.

General Performance Suggestions

The officiant, lay or ordained, must have some chanting skill. Helpful general remarks on the singing of chant may be found in the Performance Notes to *The Hymnal 1982* (Service Music pp 12–14). It is particularly important that the officiant set an example of a light and fluid style of singing from the very first versicle. The community should be encouraged to sing with particular attention to the corporate nature of singing the Office. If each person senses the breathing rhythm of those who are near by, a wonderful unity may emerge as the community sings its worship. Gentle and unforced singing is most conducive to the singing of these historic chants.

It is worth noting that in monastic communities the Daily Offices are traditionally recited in choir-wise seating; that is, with two approximately equal groups positioned facing one another across an aisle. This type of arrangement, often called a divided chancel, is well suited to the singing of the Office since it determines the two groups required for antiphonal singing of the verses of the psalms and the stanzas of the hymns. Antiphonal practice, the dividing of the singing equally between two equal groups, is not only customary but is also very practical. This practice mingles reading and singing with equal parts of listening and reflection thereby aerating the experience of worship. It heightens the rhythm of the service, creating a real dialogue within the community. Moreover, it allows a community to sing for twice as long without vocal fatigue since each member sings only half of the service.

When the psalms are sung antiphonally, it is recommended that the officiant (or a cantor) sing the first half verse—to the asterisk—as an intonation. The full community then may join to complete the first verse. Side 'A' then sings verse 2, Side 'B' sings verse 3, and so forth in alternation for the remainder of the psalm. It is customary that a pause occur at the asterisk of each verse. There is no pause between verses when the singing passes from one group to the other.

For practical purposes, it may be agreed that lines of text be sung through without rhythmic interruption for punctuation or breathing. When more than one psalm is appointed, each one may be intoned by a cantor in the manner of the first psalm and may follow without pause. At the conclusion of the entire portion of the psalter, *Gloria Patri* is sung by both sides together.

When possible, the chosen Office hymn should be sung without keyboard accompaniment. The officiant (or an appointed cantor) may establish the pitch and tempo by intoning the first line of the hymn (or as far as the first breath mark). The full community may then join the singing. It may be desirable for the stanzas of some hymns to be sung by two alternating groups, the final stanza being sung by all. Some singers may be encouraged to embellish a stanza by singing the plainsong melody a perfect fifth above or fourth below the printed pitch.

In Compline, the Antiphon "Guide us waking" may be intoned by the officiant or a cantor as far as the breath mark. The full community may then join in completing the Antiphon. The Compline service provides two settings each for "Into your hands" and "Lord, hear our prayer." In both cases the first of the two is the authentic proper chant and the second is a simpler generic versicle tone which may be substituted if necessary.

David Hurd
The General Theological Seminary
New York City, 1988

An
Order of Service
for
Noonday

Preces

Officiant

O God, make speed to save us.

People

O Lord, make haste to help us.

Officiant and People

Glory to the Father, and to the Son, and to the Holy Spi - rit:

as it was in the beginning, is now, and will be for ever. A - men.

Except in Lent, add

Al - le - lu - ia.

A suitable hymn may be sung. See Hymns 1–6

1 (13)   The golden sun lights up the sky

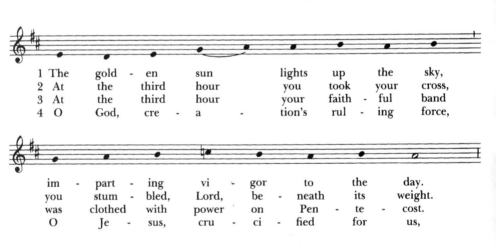

1 The gold - en sun lights up the sky,
2 At the third hour you took your cross,
3 At the third hour your faith - ful band
4 O God, cre - a - tion's rul - ing force,

im - part - ing vi - gor to the day.
you stum - bled, Lord, be - neath its weight.
was clothed with power on Pen - te - cost.
O Je - sus, cru - ci - fied for us,

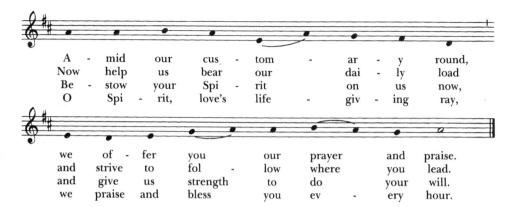

A - mid our cus - tom - ar - y round,
Now help us bear our dai - ly load
Be - stow your Spi - rit on us now,
O Spi - rit, love's life - giv - ing ray,

we of - fer you our prayer and praise.
and strive to fol - low where you lead.
and give us strength to do your will.
we praise and bless you ev - ery hour.

Words: Charles P. Price (b. 1920)
Music: *Verbum supernum prodiens,* plainsong, Mode 8, Einsiedeln MS., 13th cent.   LM

O God, creation's secret force   (15) 2

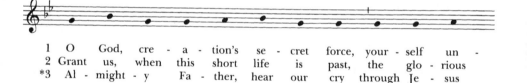

1 O God, cre - a - tion's se - cret force, your - self un -
2 Grant us, when this short life is past, the glo - rious
*3 Al - might - y Fa - ther, hear our cry through Je - sus

moved, all mo - tion's source, you, from the morn till
eve - ning that shall last; that, by a ho - ly
Christ, our Lord Most High, whom with the Spi - rit

eve - ning's ray, through all its chan - ges guide the day:
death at - tained, e - ter - nal glo - ry may be gained.
we a - dore for ev - er and for ev - er - more.

Words: Ambrose of Milan (340-397); tr. John Mason Neale (1818-1866), alt.
      St. 3, James Waring McCrady (b. 1938)
Music: *Te lucis ante terminum,* plainsong, Mode 8, *Antiphonale Sarisburiense,* vol. II   LM

3 (16)   **Now let us sing our praise to God**

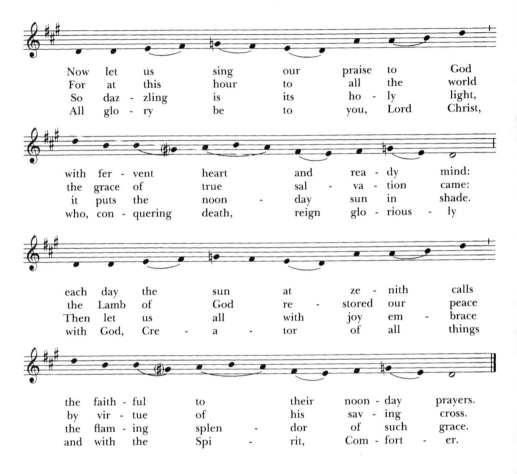

Now   let   us   sing   our   praise   to   God
For   at   this   hour   to   all   the   world
So   daz - zling   is   its   ho - ly   light,
All   glo - ry   be   to   you,   Lord   Christ,

with   fer - vent   heart   and   rea - dy   mind:
the   grace of   true   sal -   va - tion   came:
it   puts   the   noon - day   sun   in   shade.
who,   con - quering death,   reign   glo - rious -   ly

each   day   the   sun   at   ze - nith   calls
the   Lamb   of   God   re -   stored our   peace
Then   let   us   all   with   joy   em -   brace
with   God,   Cre - a   -   tor   of   all   things

the   faith - ful   to   their   noon - day   prayers.
by   vir - tue   of   his   sav - ing   cross.
the   flam - ing   splen - dor   of   such   grace.
and   with   the   Spi -   rit,   Com - fort -   er.

Words: Latin; ver. *Hymnal 1982*. St. 4, Anne K. LeCroy (b. 1930)
Music: *Dicamus laudes Domino*, plainsong, Mode 5, Nevers MS., 13th cent.   LM

4 (18)   **As now the sun shines down at noon**

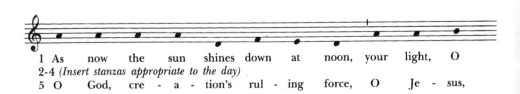

1 As   now   the   sun   shines down   at   noon,   your   light,   O
2-4 *(Insert stanzas appropriate to the day)*
5 O   God,   cre - a -   tion's rul - ing   force, O   Je -   sus,

4   Noonday

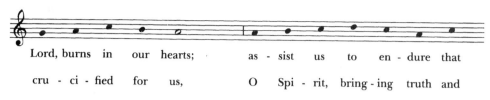

Lord, burns in our hearts; as - sist us to en - dure that
cru - ci - fied for us, O Spi - rit, bring - ing truth and

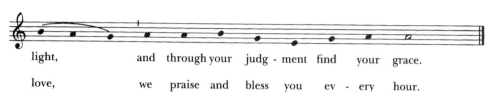

light, and through your judg - ment find your grace.
love, we praise and bless you ev - ery hour.

Monday and Thursday

2 The sun stood still for Joshua
while he contended, Lord, for you;
so may we struggle faithfully
and seek our victory in your peace.

3 At noon you hung upon the cross
betrayed, forsaken, all alone;
help us to share your pain and grief,
and, sharing, know life's victory won.

4 At noon you came to Jacob's well,
athirst and spent, you asked for aid;
to us, like her who saw your need,
your living water give to drink.

Tuesday and Saturday

2 Elijah taunted Baal at noon;
he knew you, Lord, would answer him;
may we, too, trust your sovereign power
when we must act in day's hard light.

3 On Golgotha the sky turned dark;
all shadows of the morn and eve
converged to shield frail human eyes
from all the woe you bore for us.

4 At noontime Paul beheld your light,
so bright it cancelled out the sun;
you blinded and converted him:
O turn us now to see your face.

Wednesday and Friday

2 By noon's bright light, destruction stalks;
ten thousand perish at our side;
held by your unrelenting grace,
let us cling always to your love.

3 The dark midday could not conceal
your cry of awful agony;
teach us to hear its echoes still
in every human misery.

4 In noonday vision Peter saw
that all you made was pure and clean;
grant us that same revealing light
that we may see your world is good.

Words: Charles P. Price (b. 1920) and Carl P. Daw, Jr. (b. 1944)
Music: *Jesu dulcis memoria*, plainsong, Mode 2   LM

Now Holy Spirit, ever One

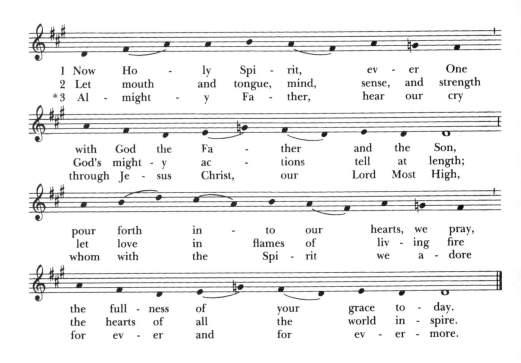

1 Now Ho - ly Spi - rit, ev - er One
2 Let mouth and tongue, mind, sense, and strength
*3 Al - might - y Fa - ther, hear our cry

with God the Fa - ther and the Son,
God's might - y ac - tions tell at length;
through Je - sus Christ, our Lord Most High,

pour forth in - to our hearts, we pray,
let love in flames of liv - ing fire
whom with the Spi - rit we a - dore

the full - ness of your grace to - day.
the hearts of all the world in - spire.
for ev - er and for ev - er - more.

Words: Ambrose of Milan (340-397); ver. *Hymnal 1982*. St. 3, James Waring McCrady (b. 1938)
Music: *Nunc Sancte nobis Spiritus*, plainsong, Mode 5, Verona MS., 12th cent.

LM

O God of truth, O Lord of might

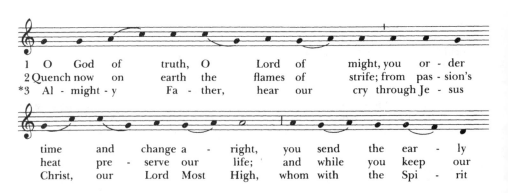

1 O God of truth, O Lord of might, you or - der
2 Quench now on earth the flames of strife; from pas - sion's
*3 Al - might - y Fa - ther, hear our cry through Je - sus

time and change a - right, you send the ear - ly
heat pre - serve our life; and while you keep our
Christ, our Lord Most High, whom with the Spi - rit

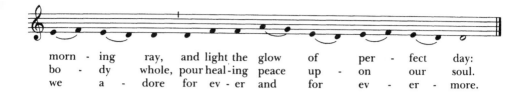

morn - ing	ray,	and light the	glow	of	per - fect	day:
bo - dy	whole,	pour heal - ing	peace	up - on	our	soul.
we a - dore	for ev - er	and	for	ev - er - more.

Words: Ambrose of Milan (340–397); ver. *Hymnal 1982.* St. 3, James Waring McCrady (b. 1938)

Music: *Nunc Sancte nobis Spiritus,* plainsong, Mode 5, Engelberg MS., 14th cent.

LM

One or more of the following Psalms is sung. Other suitable selections include Psalms 19, 67, one or more selections from Psalm 119, or a selection from Psalms 120 through 133.

Psalm 119   *Lucerna pedibus meis*

Tone 8

105   *Your word* is a lantern to my féet *
     and a / light up - ón my path.

106   I have sworn and am detérmined *
     to keep your / righteous júdgments.

107   I am deeply tróubled; *
     preserve my life, O Lord, ac-/cording tó your word.

108   Accept, O Lord, the willing tribute of my líps, *
     and teach / me your júdgments.

109   My life is always in my hánd, *
     yet I do / not forgét your law.

110   The wicked have set a tráp for me, *
     but I have not strayed from / your commándments.

111   Your decrees are my inheritance for éver; *
     truly, they are the / joy of mý heart.

112   I have applied my heart to fulfill your státutes *
     for ev- / er and to the end.

Psalm 121   *Levavi oculos*

Tone 8

1   *I lift* up my eyes to the hílls; *
    From where / is my hélp to come?

2   My help comes from the Lórd, *
    the ma-/ker of héaven and earth.

3   He will not let your foot be móved *
    and he who watches òver you / will not fáll asleep.

4   Behold, he who keeps watch òver Ísrael *
    shall neither / slumber nór sleep;

5   The Lord himself watches óver you; *
    the Lord is your shade / at your ríght hand,

6   So that the sun shall not strike you by dáy *
    — / nor the móon by night.

7   The Lord shall preserve you from all évil; *
    it is he / who shall kéep you safe.

8   The Lord shall watch over you going out and your cóming in, *
    from this time / forth for évermore.

Psalm 126   *In convertendo*

Tone 8

1   *When the* Lord restored the fortunes of Zíon, *
    then were / we like thóse who dream.

2   Then was our mouth filled with laúghter, *
    and our / tongue with shóuts of joy.

3   Then they said among the nátions, *
    "The Lord has / done great thíngs for them."

4   The Lord has done great thíngs for us, *
    and / we are glád indeed.

5   Restore our fortunes, O Lórd, *
    like the watercourses / of the Négev.

6 Those who sowed with téars *
   will / reap with sóngs of joy.

7 Those who go out weeping, carrying the séed, *
   will come again with joy, / shouldering their sheaves.

At the end of the Psalms, or after each Psalm is sung

Tone 8

Glory to the Father, and to the Són, *
   and to the / Holy Spírit: *

As it was in the beginning, is nów, *
   and will be for / ever. Ámen.

One of the following, or some other suitable passage of Scripture, is sung or read.

Romans 5:5

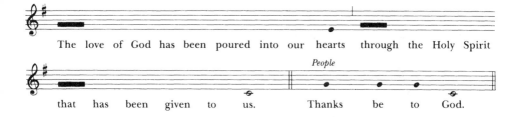

The love of God has been poured into our hearts through the Holy Spirit

People

that has been given to us. Thanks be to God.

2 Corinthians 5:17-18

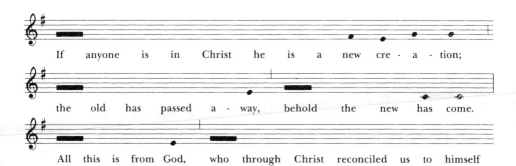

If anyone is in Christ he is a new cre - a - tion;

the old has passed a - way, behold the new has come.

All this is from God, who through Christ reconciled us to himself

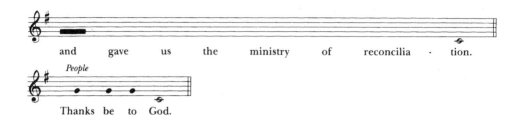

and gave us the ministry of reconcilia · tion.

People

Thanks be to God.

Malachi 1:11

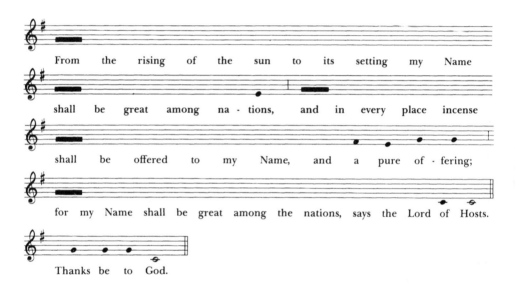

From the rising of the sun to its setting my Name

shall be great among na · tions, and in every place incense

shall be offered to my Name, and a pure of · fering;

for my Name shall be great among the nations, says the Lord of Hosts.

Thanks be to God.

A meditation, silent or spoken, may follow.

The Officiant then begins the Prayers.

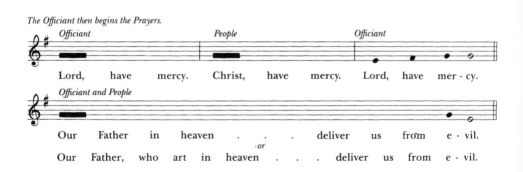

Officiant   *People*   *Officiant*

Lord, have mercy.   Christ, have mercy.   Lord, have mer · cy.

Officiant and People

Our Father in heaven . . . deliver us from e · vil.

or

Our Father, who art in heaven . . . deliver us from e · vil.

Lord, hear our prayer; And let our cry come to you. Let us pray.

The Officiant then sings one of the Collects appointed. If desired, the Collect of the Day may be used. The Collect may be monotoned or sung to Collect Tone I, page 30.

Heavenly Father, send your Holy Spirit into our hearts, to direct and rule us according to your will, to comfort us in all our afflictions, to defend us from all error, and to lead us into all truth, through Jesus Christ our Lord. *Amen.*

Blessed Saviour, at this hour you hung upon the cross, stretching out your loving arms: Grant that all the peoples of the earth may look to you and be saved; for your tender mercies' sake. *Amen.*

Almighty Saviour, who at noonday called your servant Saint Paul to be an apostle to the Gentiles: We pray you to illumine the world with the radiance of your glory, that all nations may come and worship you; for you live and reign for ever and ever. *Amen.*

Lord Jesus Christ, you said to your apostles, "Peace I give to you; my own peace I leave with you:" Regard not our sins, but the faith of your Church, and give to us the peace and unity of that heavenly City, where with the Father and the Holy Spirit you live and reign, now and for ever. *Amen.*

Free intercessions may be offered.

The service concludes as follows.

Let us bless the Lord. Thanks be to God.

Noonday setting: Ver. *Hymnal 1982*

An
Order
for
Compline

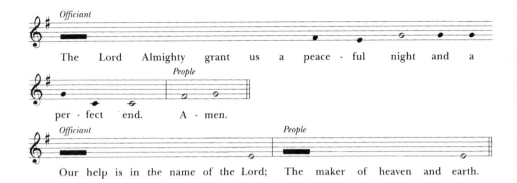

The Lord Almighty grant us a peace - ful night and a per - fect end. A - men.

Our help is in the name of the Lord; The maker of heaven and earth.

The Office continues with "O God, make speed to save us," or with the following Confession of Sin.

Officiant
Let us confess our sins to God.

Silence may be kept.

Officiant and People
Almighty God, our heavenly Father:
We have sinned against you,
through our own fault,
in thought, and word, and deed,
and in what we have left undone.
For the sake of your Son our Lord Jesus Christ,
Forgive us all our offenses;
and grant that we may serve you
in newness of life,
to the glory of your Name. Amen.

Officiant
May the Almighty God grant us forgiveness of all our sins,
and the grace and comfort of the Holy Spirit. *Amen.*

O God, make speed to save us. O Lord, make haste to help us.

Glory to the Father, and to the Son, and to the Holy Spi - rit:

as it was in the beginning, is now, and will be for ever. A - men.

Except in Lent, add:

Al - le - lu - ia.

One or more of the following Psalms are sung. Other suitable selections may be substituted.

Psalm 4   *Cum invocarem*

Tone 8

1   *Answer me* when I call, O God, defender of my cáuse; *
     you set me free when I am hard-pressed;
     have mercy on / me and héar my prayer.

2   "You mortals, how long will you dishonor my glóry? *
     how long will you worship dumb idols
     and run / after fálse gods?"

3   Know that the Lord does wonders for the fáithful; *
     when I call upon the Lord, / he will héar me.

4   Tremble, then, and dó not sin; *
     speak to your heart in si- / lence upón your bed.

5   Offer the appointed sacrifíces, *
     and put your / trust in thé Lord.

6   Many are saying, "Oh, that we might see bétter times!" *
     Lift up the light of your countenance up - /on us, Ó Lord.

7   You have put gladness in my héart, *
     more than when grain and / wine and óil increase.

8   I lie down in peace; at once I fáll asleep; *
     for only you, Lord, make me / dwell in sáfety.

Psalm 31 *In te, Domine, speravi*

Tone 8

1   *In you,* O Lord, have I taken refuge;
let me never be púk to shame; *
    deliver me / in your ríghteousness.

2   Incline your eár to me; *
    make haste / to delíver me.

3   Be my strong rock, a castle to keep me safe,
for you are my crag and my strónghold; *
    for the sake of your Name, lead / me and guíde me.

4   Take me out of the net that they have secretly sét for me, *
    for you / are my tówer of strength.

5   Into your hands I commend my spírit, *
    for you have redeemed me,
    O / Lord, O Gód of truth.

Psalm 91 *Qui habitat*

Tone 8

1   *He who* dwells in the shelter of the Móst High *
    abides under the shadow of / the Almíghty.

2   He shall say to the Lord,
"You are my refuge and my strónghold, *
    my God in / whom I púk my trust."

3   He shall deliver you from the snare of the húnter *
    and from the / deadly péstilence.

4   He shall cover you with his pinions,
and you shall find refuge under his wíngs; *
    his faithfulness shall be a / shield and búckler.

5   You shall not be afraid of any terror by níght, *
    nor of the ar- / row that flíes by day;

6   Of the plague that stalks in the dárkness, *
    nor of the sickness that lays / waste at míd-day.

7 A thousand shall fall at your side
   and ten thousand at your ríght hand, *
      but it shall / not come néar you.

8 Your eyes have only to behóld *
      to see the reward / of the wícked.

9 Because you have made the Lord your réfuge, *
      and the Most High your / habitátion,

10 There shall no evil happen to yóu, *
      neither shall any plague come / near your dwélling.

11 For he shall give his angels charge óver you, *
      to keep / you in áll your ways.

12 They shall bear you in their hánds, *
      lest you dash your / foot agaínst a stone.

13 You shall tread upon the lion and ádder; *
      you shall trample the young lion and the serpent / under yóur feet.

14 Because he is bound to me in love,
   therefore will I delíver him; *
      I will protect him, be- / cause he knóws my Name.

15 He shall call upon me, and I will ánswer him; *
      I am with him in trouble;
      I will rescue him and bring / him to hónor.

16 With long life will I satisfý him, *
      and show him / my salvátion.

Psalm 134   *Ecce nunc*

Tone 8

1 *Be-hold now,* bless the Lord, all you servants of the Lórd, *
      you that stand by night in the / house of thé Lord.

2 Lift up your hands in the holy place and bléss the Lord; *
      the Lord who made heaven and earth bless you / out of Zíon.

Tone 8

Glory to the Father, and to the Són *
and to the / Holy Spírit:

As it was in the beginning, is nów *
and will be for / ever. Ámen.

One of the following, or some other suitable passage of Scripture, is sung or read

Jeremiah 14:9, 22

Lord, you are in the midst of us, and we are called

by your Name: Do not forsake us, O Lord our God.

People

Thanks be to God.

or the following

Matthew 11:28-30

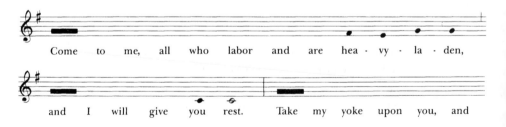

Come to me, all who labor and are hea - vy - la - den,

and I will give you rest. Take my yoke upon you, and

learn from me; For I am gentle and lowly in heart,
and you will find rest for your souls. For my yoke is easy,
and my burden is light.

People

Thanks be to God.

Hebrews 13:20-21

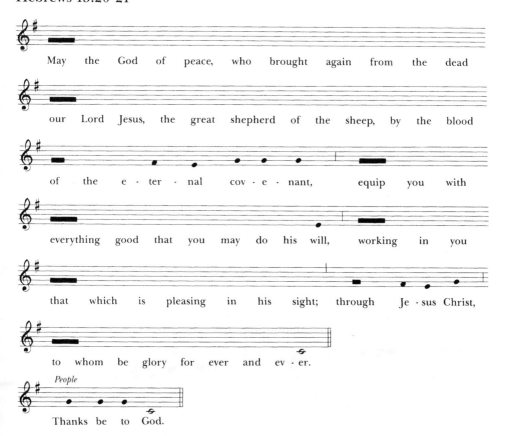

May the God of peace, who brought again from the dead
our Lord Jesus, the great shepherd of the sheep, by the blood
of the e - ter - nal cov - e - nant, equip you with
everything good that you may do his will, working in you
that which is pleasing in his sight; through Je - sus Christ,
to whom be glory for ever and ev - er.

People

Thanks be to God.

1 Peter 5: 8-9a

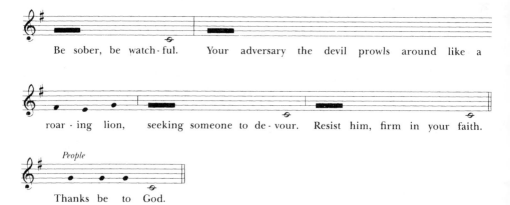

Be sober, be watch-ful. Your adversary the devil prowls around like a

roar - ing lion, seeking someone to de - vour. Resist him, firm in your faith.

People

Thanks be to God.

A hymn suitable for the evening may be sung. See Hymns 7–11

7 (38)　　　　　　　　　　　　　　　　　Jesus, Redeemer of the world

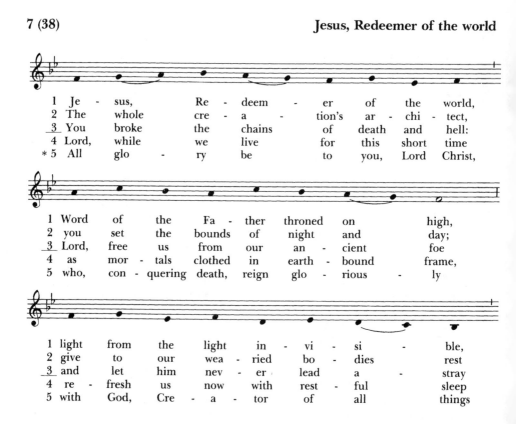

1	Je - sus,		Re - deem		- er	of	the	world,
2	The	whole	cre - a		- tion's	ar - chi - tect,		
3	You	broke	the	chains	of	death	and	hell:
4	Lord,	while	we	live	for	this	short	time
*5	All	glo - ry		be	to	you,	Lord	Christ,

1	Word	of	the	Fa - ther		throned	on		high,
2	you	set	the	bounds	of	night	and		day;
3	Lord,	free	us	from	our	an - cient			foe
4	as	mor - tals		clothed	in	earth - bound			frame,
5	who,	con - quering		death,	reign	glo - rious		-	ly

1	light	from	the	light	in - vi - si			-	ble,
2	give	to	our	wea - ried		bo - dies			rest
3	and	let	him	nev - er		lead	a	-	stray
4	re - fresh		us	now	with	rest - ful			sleep
5	with	God,	Cre - a - tor			of	all		things

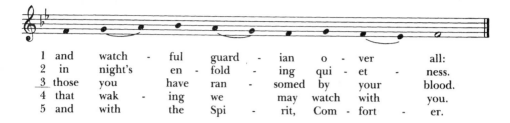

Words: Latin, 10th cent.; ver *Hymnal 1982.* St. 5, Anne K. LeCroy (b. 1930)
Music: *Jesu, nostra redemptio,* plainsong, Mode 8, Worcester MS., 13th cent.　　　　LM

O Christ, you are both light and day　　　　(40) 8

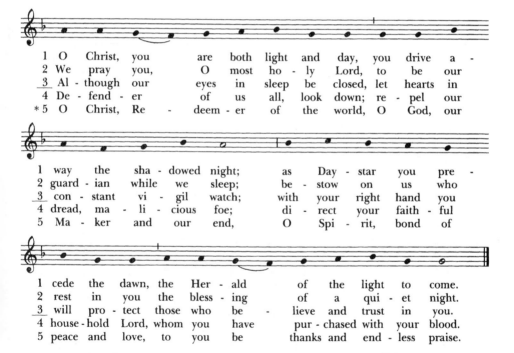

Words: Latin, 6th cent.; ver. *Hymnal 1982.* St. 5, Charles P. Price (b. 1920)
Music: *Christe, qui Lux es et dies,* plainsong, Mode 2, *Mailander Hymnen,* 15th cent.　　　　LM

All praise to thee, my God, this night

1 All praise to thee, my God, this night, for all the bless-ings of the light: keep me, O keep me, King of kings, be-neath thine own al-might-y wings.

2 For-give me, Lord, for thy dear Son, the ill that I this day have done; that with the world, my-self, and thee, I, ere I sleep, at peace may be.

3 O may my soul on thee re-pose, and with sweet sleep mine eye-lids close; sleep that shall me more vi-gorous make to serve my God when I a-wake.

4 Praise God, from whom all bless-ings flow; praise him, all crea-tures here be-low; praise him a-bove, ye heaven-ly host: praise Fa-ther, Son, and Ho-ly Ghost.

This hymn may be sung as a four-part canon at the distance of one measure.

Words: Thomas Ken (1637-1711)
Music: *The Eighth Tune*, Thomas Tallis (1505?-1585)

LM

To you before the close of day

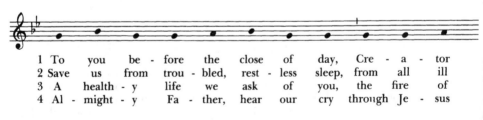

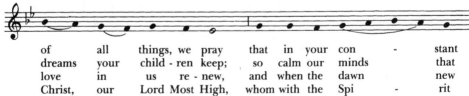

1 To you be-fore the close of day, Cre-a-tor of all things, we pray that in your con - stant

2 Save us from trou-bled, rest-less sleep, from all ill dreams your child-ren keep; so calm our minds that

3 A health-y life we ask of you, the fire of love in us re-new, and when the dawn new

4 Al-might-y Fa-ther, hear our cry through Je-sus Christ, our Lord Most High, whom with the Spi - rit

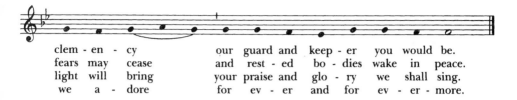

clem - en - cy	our guard and	keep - er	you would be.
fears may cease	and rest - ed	bo - dies	wake in peace.
light will bring	your praise and	glo - ry	we shall sing.
we a - dore	for ev - er	and for	ev - er - more.

Words: Latin, 6th cent.; ver. *Hymnal 1982*. St. 4, James Waring McCrady (b. 1938)
Music: *Te lucis ante terminum*, plainsong, Mode 8, *Antiphonale Sarisburiense*, vol. II   LM

To you before the close of day   (45) 11

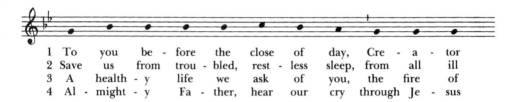

1 To you be - fore the close of day, Cre - a - tor
2 Save us from trou - bled, rest - less sleep, from all ill
3 A health - y life we ask of you, the fire of
4 Al - might - y Fa - ther, hear our cry through Je - sus

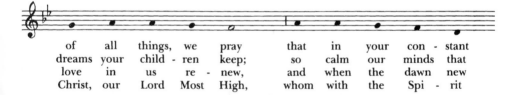

of all things, we pray that in your con - stant
dreams your child - ren keep; so calm our minds that
love in us re - new, and when the dawn new
Christ, our Lord Most High, whom with the Spi - rit

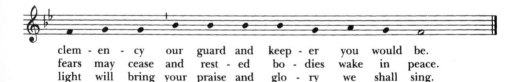

clem - en - cy our guard and keep - er you would be.
fears may cease and rest - ed bo - dies wake in peace.
light will bring your praise and glo - ry we shall sing.
we a - dore for ev - er and for ev - er - more.

Words: Latin, 6th cent.; ver. *Hymnal 1982*. St. 4, James Waring McCrady (b. 1938)
Music: *Te lucis ante terminum*, plainsong, Mode 8   LM

Responsory: Into your hands

Versicle: Into your hands

This setting may be used in place of the preceding.

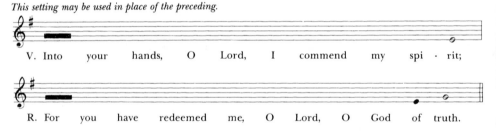

Then follows

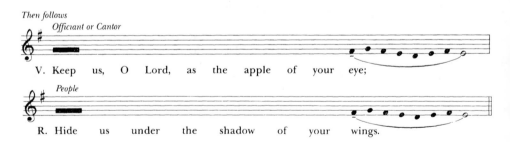

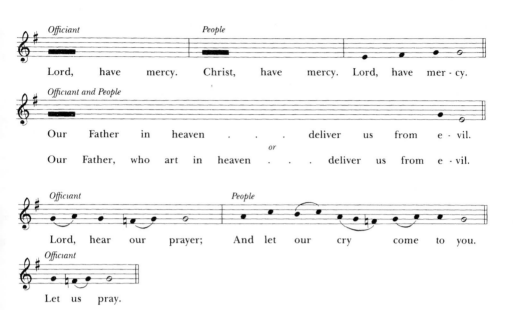

Lord, have mercy. Christ, have mercy. Lord, have mer-cy.

Officiant and People

Our Father in heaven . . . deliver us from e-vil.

or

Our Father, who art in heaven . . . deliver us from e-vil.

Lord, hear our prayer; And let our cry come to you.

Let us pray.

This setting may be used in place of the preceding.

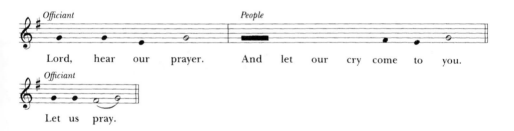

Lord, hear our prayer. And let our cry come to you.

Let us pray.

The Collect may be monotoned or sung to Collect Tone I, page 30.

Be our light in the darkness, O Lord, and in your great mercy defend us from all perils and dangers of this night; for the love of your only Son, our Savior Jesus Christ. *Amen.*

Be present, O merciful God, and protect us through the hours of this night, so that we who are wearied by the changes and chances of this life may rest in your eternal changelessness; through Jesus Christ our Lord. *Amen.*

Look down, O Lord, from your heavenly throne, and illumine this night with your celestial brightness; that by night as by day your people may glorify your holy Name; through Jesus Christ our Lord. *Amen.*

Visit this place, O Lord, and drive far from it all snares of the enemy; let your holy angels dwell with us to preserve us in peace; and let your blessings be upon us always; through Jesus Christ our Lord. *Amen.*

A Collect for Saturdays

We give you thanks, O God, for revealing your Son Jesus Christ to us by the light of his resurrection: Grant that as we sing your glory at the close of this day, our joy may abound in the morning as we celebrate the Paschal mystery; through Jesus Christ our Lord. *Amen.*

One of the following prayers may be added

Keep watch, dear Lord, with those who work, or watch, or weep this night, and give your angels charge over those who sleep. Tend the sick, Lord Christ, give rest to the weary, bless the dying, soothe the suffering, pity the afflicted, shield the joyous, and all for your love's sake. *Amen.*

or this

O God, your unfailing providence sustains the world we live in and the life we live: Watch over those, both night and day, who work while others sleep, and grant that we may never forget that our common life depends upon each other's toil; through Jesus Christ our Lord. *Amen.*

The Song of Simeon   *Nunc dimittis*

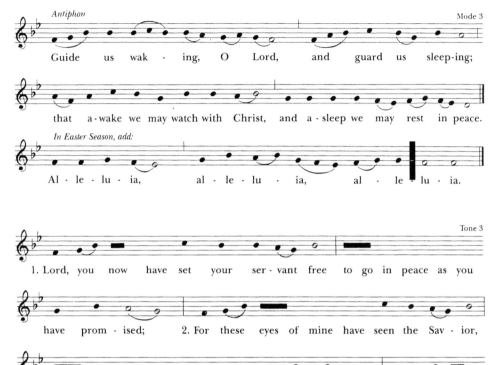

Antiphon   Mode 3

Guide us wak - ing, O Lord, and guard us sleep-ing;

that a - wake we may watch with Christ, and a - sleep we may rest in peace.

In Easter Season, add:

Al - le - lu - ia, al - le - lu - ia, al - le - lu - ia.

Tone 3

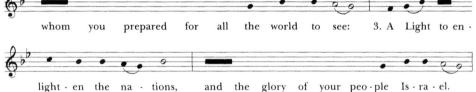

1. Lord, you now have set your ser - vant free to go in peace as you

have prom - ised; 2. For these eyes of mine have seen the Sav - ior,

whom you prepared for all the world to see: 3. A Light to en -

light - en the na - tions, and the glory of your peo - ple Is - ra - el.

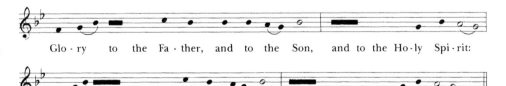

Glo - ry to the Fa - ther, and to the Son, and to the Ho - ly Spi - rit:

as it was in the be - gin - ning, is now, and will be for ev - er. A - men. [Ant.]

Concluding Versicle and Blessing

Let us bless the Lord.   Thanks be to God.

The almighty and mer-ci-ful Lord, Father, Son, and Holy Spi-rit,

bless us and keep us.   A-men.

Compline Setting: adapt. David Hurd (b. 1950)

Appendix

Collect Tone I

The flex is used at the end of the opening phrase, if it is long enough; otherwise it is omitted. Cadence I and cadence II are used at the ends of significant phrases within the prayer. One or both of the cadences is repeated when the length of the prayer permits. In both cadences, the movement from one pitch to another takes place on a heavily accented syllable.

Collects which have a long ending are concluded as follows: flex (on the phrase "through Jesus Christ our Lord"), cadence II, cadence I.

Collects which have a short ending are concluded with cadence I.

Collect of 2 Epiphany: Tone I

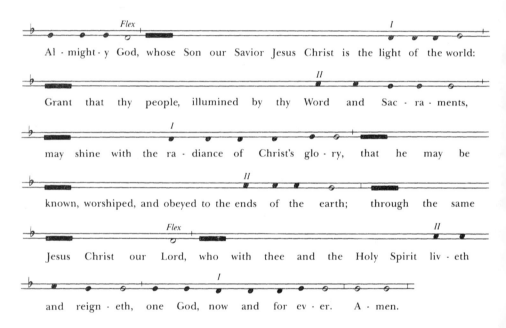

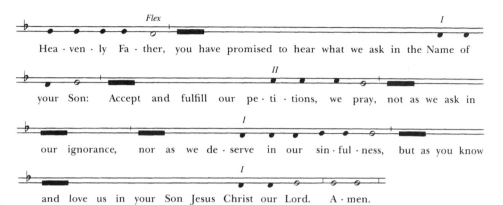

Hea - ven - ly Fa - ther, you have promised to hear what we ask in the Name of

your Son: Accept and fulfill our pe - ti - tions, we pray, not as we ask in

our ignorance, nor as we de - serve in our sin - ful - ness, but as you know

and love us in your Son Jesus Christ our Lord. A - men.